Also by Eric Hoffman

POETRY

Forms of Life (2015)
By the Hours (2013)
The American Eye (2011)

PROSE
(with Dominick Grace)

Seth: Conversations (2015)
Chester Brown: Conversations (2013)
Dave Sim: Conversations (2013)

THE
TRANSPARENT
EYE

Eric Hoffman

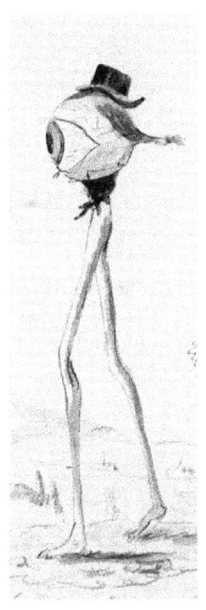

SPUYTEN DUYVIL
New York City

Certain of these poems were previously published in *BlazeVOX*, *Caliban Online*, *Country Music*, *E-Ratio*, *Indefinite Space*, *Listenlight*, *M58*, *Marsh Hawk Review*, *Moria*, *New Mystics*, *Of/with*, *Offcourse*, *Otoliths*, *Reconfigurations*, *The Tony Frazer Festschrift*, and *Ygradsil*. Additionally, a number of the poems from *Emerson In Europe* were previously published, in somewhat different form, in *The American Eye* (Dos Madres Press, 2011).

Primary text: Ralph Waldo Emerson, *Selected Journals* 1820-1842, Lawrence Rosenwald, ed. (Library of America, 2010).

© 2016 Eric Hoffman
ISBN 978-1-941550-92-2

Cover image: Christopher Pearse Cranch, c. 1840. "Standing on the bare ground—my head/bathed by the blithe air, & uplifted into/ infinite space—all mean egotism vanishes./I become a transparent Eyeball." Inscribed in ink bottom right: "I expand, and live in/the warm day, like corn/and melons." Emerson, *Nature* (13)

Library of Congress Cataloging-in-Publication Data

Names: Hoffman, Eric R., author.
Title: The transparent eye / Eric Hoffman.
Description: New York City : Spuyten Duyvil, [2016]
Identifiers: LCCN 2015044654 | ISBN 9781941550922
Classification: LCC PS3608.O47767 A6 2016 | DDC 811/.6--dc23
LC record available at http://lccn.loc.gov/2015044654

for Robin and Sailor

Contents

Emerson In Europe 1

Emerson In America 79

EMERSON IN EUROPE

If the whole of history is in one man, it is all to be explained from individual experience. There is a relation between the hours of our life and the centuries of time. As the air I breathe is drawn from the great repositories of nature, as the light on my book is yielded by a star a hundred million of miles distant, as the poise of my body depends on the equilibrium of centrifugal and centripetal forces, so the hours should be instructed by the ages and the ages explained by the hours. Of the universal mind each individual man is one more incarnation. All its properties consist in him. Every step in his private experience flashes a light on what great bodies of men have done, and the crises of his life refer to national crises. Every revolution was first a thought in one man's mind, and when the same thought occurs to another man, it is the key to that era.

RALPH WALDO EMERSON, *History*

Set sail, Christmas Day, 1832.
Sick at first. The sea is rough.

Assemble *Lycidas* from memory
Like Isis Osiris' broken body.

Once the storm eases,
Spend long hours on deck,

Learning to use the sextant,
Lamenting my poor knowledge of the sea,

Of geometry & astronomy.
Drawing conclusions from everything:

The voyage a metaphor for life,
Rich with sentiment & symbol.

Freedom. Inside, terrible freedom.
Outside, thousands of laws,
Of physics & of men.
But inside, that temptation
Overruns us, rendering the soul
A plaything for vice,
Tarnishing the white walls
Of our reputations.

My ministry in tatters,
My Ellen now so sadly altered.
Where I encountered a chilling fear
She expected serenity
Even when her every breath
Offered her distress. & now
The invisible multitude of all
Breathing things becomes
A silent choir.

My eye is American.
Like a chemist assembling substances
I bring myself to sea
In search of affinities –

The bubble
By its birthright – expands –
& my American eye
Is like a child's again.

24 November 1832.
Died my sister Margaret Tucker.
Farewell, dear girl.
We anchor upon a few.

Teach me to make trifles,
Trifles & work with consistency –
Pass on, pure Soul!
To the opening of heaven.

What I am in words, I am in life.
To be genuine, one's ambition
Must be proportional to one's powers,
The pinnacle determining
The breadth of its base –

No one teaches the heart.
Instead they find themselves
Insisting upon great truths,
Showing them to be agreeable –
This cripples the teaching

& bereaves reality. Its force
Is something secondary
& cannot stand alone.
The truth of truth consists in this,
self-evident, subsistent. It is light.

I write empty sentences
In my journal. In death
Words become poor company.
I expect more from them
Than they have to offer.

We search desolation
For healing & for peace
As if they are mis-placed objects.

"Teach me I am forgotten by the dead
& the dead is by herself forgotten."

Retreat into reading:
Plotinus. The Bible.
Did Matthew, Mark, Luke & John exist?
When all else falls into ruin

Their lonely words
Cry out faith
In the wilderness.

Landor's Epicurus: "I teach by degrees."
Not the will, but the necessity of the wise.
One knows there is an error,
Yet hasn't found its boundary.

"The mighty tread brings dust from the sound of liberty"–
"The true Philosophy is the only true Prophet" –

There is truth enough to open the mind's door,
To straighten the passages. There is power
Enough & there is happiness.

That which delights shall be Good.

Forever I forego the yoke of men's opinions,
For in the darkest maze amid the sweetest baits,
The needle meanders north, the little bird
Remembers its notes.

I never taught what it teaches me.
I only follow when I act aright.

New tongues repeat old proverbs,
Primeval truths. The thought occurred,
Full of consolation, that if man
Touches the severest truth, he admits
To himself the existence of God –
A strict soliloquy in absolute solitude –
The soul a hermit in creation.

In such a state, the question
Of whether your boat shall float
Or sink to the bottom is of no more importance
Than the flight of a snow-flake.

Why must I travel across the sea?
Under the lee of the spencer sheet
I find a solitary thoughtful hour –

The vast envelope of sky
Lit by the same light that illuminates
Distant shores, painted canvases,

Carved marbles, renowned towns –
These places & names
From childhood.

The thing set down in words is not affirmed.
It must affirm itself:
This is the core of the world.

I would lie in her tomb
Should God accept
This miserable replacement –

Will the beam of her eye
Ever trace this stained visage
Whose cheeks are burned
By sour tears?

Poor poetry cannot resolve this lone heart
Which stutters & fails –

"It is a luxury to be understood."

The voyage at sea is such a bundle of perils
That only the lover of the present
Would be swift to pay the price
For any commodity which anything else would buy –

Yet should our horses be somewhat mild
& our roads uneven & lonely without inns,
The coward eye still magnifies every danger.

In the wonderful store of memory
We carry power & peace –
A monument of high antiquity.

The pyramids' sides cannot contain
The story of half so much time,
Or be inscribed with the magic
Of its myriad-fold methods –

Its order comprehends a thousand lines –
Every point lives, & its center
Or extreme in turn.

As lightning shines out of one part of heaven
So one thought in this firmament
Flashes light over the sphere.

Man sees himself as the result
Of blind circumstance,
His internals evanescent opal shades.

Let him turn the telescope around,
Let him be compared with durable things.

He will find that they outshine
All categories of defect or shame,
All technical, metaphysical or practical art,
& belong to the great All
Into which all are born.

A long & wild storm
Consigns us to darkness & nausea –
Helpless, we cling to hope
& memory of firmer ground –

The sailor is a man of his hands,
Eye, muscle, finger. He is a tailor,
Carpenter, copper, stevedore,
Clerk & astronomer,
Guide & savior –

The Captain speaks of the superiority
Of the American to the European,
Yet light shines equally in either place,
It smiles equally on time & space,
It diminishes & enlarges until both
Are of equal size. It breathes life
Into man & man into life.

Wandering the Green Mountains
& Lake Champlaign, June 1831,
Finding you nowhere & everywhere,
Translating symbols into sentiments.

We grow wise. We search for what is similar
In ourselves; an equal appreciation
For byson tea or a walk before breakfast.

What is it in me that cannot say I do not know?
"The noblest eye is darkened"
& Galileo went blind 1636, died 1642.
So the eye of Milton.

"29 March. I visited Ellen's tomb
& opened the coffin"

O wilted apple –
Who can discern your gentle rage
In his own heart?

A hollowness fades –

At times I think
The true prerequisite of ministry
Is the urge for antiquity,
An altered age
Where one worships
Dead forms, concealing
A secret pursuit
Of Pagany –

When we read we acquire
A crystallization of ourselves –
These books of science,
How the mind can achieve communion.

It is only the body, the blood –
A sentiment translated into symbol,
A symbol transmuted into sentiment.

Is this a new life? Or a new failure.

A prophet warms
Candles of ignorance.
Amongst his books
The dim light
Renders them illegible.

What is truth? That which cannot
Not be seen.

Even on the smallest scales
The strong lens is trained

On its furthest star,
Or the thin horizon remains fixed,

Even as the world turns its music,
Unperturbed by the massive silence of space.

Dr. Johnson rightly defends
Conversation upon the weather.
With more reason we at sea
Beat that topic thin.
We are pensioners of the wind.
The weathercock is the wisest man.
Should the wind forget to blow,
We must eat our masts.

Now we all await a smoother sea
To stand at our toilette,
Pleased that there is a time
For all things under the moon,
So that no man need give
A dinner party in a brig's cabin
Nor shave himself by gulf lightening.

I am without skill
As much at sea as on land.
My ignorance astonishes me.
How little I comprehend this world,
Which seems to me a millstone.

Like this ship, I hope & drift,
Yet this ship will, God willing,
Reach shore, whereas
I am a shipwreck continually sinking,
Only to rise to the surface
& sink once again.

I know so little of history
Or of metaphysics
& must profess myself
The poorest of philosophers.

I am pale from all my idle hours
Spent staring at a book
From which it is impossible to learn –

Imagine if this captain had only
A text to tell him of the sea,
We'd never reach our destination.

The only benefit of my ignorance
Is the affection it affords me
Of the wise, who revel in displaying
Superior knowledge.

"It occurred forcibly this morning that the thing set down in words is not affirmed. It must affirm itself or no form of grammar & no verisimilitude can give it evidence. This is a maxim which holds the core of the world."

The laws of composition –

The word is either right
Or wrong & in this
Language fails the mind's ambiguity –

The lathe of heaven
Merely a horn on one's head.

Another day as beautiful as ever
Shines on the monotonous sea,
& all the minstrelsy of nature rings,

A capricious shell, sometimes mute as wood,
A marine archetype
That murmurs when there is already noise.

The water is warm to the hands,
& far below you see motes of light by day
& streams of fire by night.

A thought, a design:
A lecture on God's architecture,
A sketch of a winter's day
As a microcosm of the cosmos –

Or to go south again
To the West Indies
For the climate.

Instead, on the spur
Of a moment, sailed east
For southern Europe,

Sold the house
& all my furniture
At auction, "that domestic
Crack of doom
& type of all forlornness."

The day is sad

The night is careful

The heart is leaded down

That exact justice is done

That the soul is immortal

That the best is true

That the mind discerns all

& seeks itself in all things

The sailor in the crow's nest
Cries out land yet each time
Is mistaken: either an illusion
Or a cloud covers his vision.

No word suits the sea like hope.
Every sign fails.

A man can guide a ship
3,000 miles to a tiny inland sea
9 miles wide with nothing more
Than the sun, a chart, &
A three cornered bit of wood –

Miracles are ubiquitous.

(Sea shanty)

Well, blithe traveler, what cheer?
What have the sea & stars
& mounting winds
& discontented thoughts sung
In your attentive ears?

The slumbering old giant
Cannot bestir himself
To loom up for the past time
Of his upstart grandchildren
As they come now,

Shoal after shoal
To salute their old progenitor
The old Adam of all.
Sleep on, old sire,
There is muscle & nerve

& enterprise in us now,
Your poor spawn
Who have sucked the air
& ripened in the sunshine
Of the cold west,

To steer our ships
To your very ports & thrust
Our inquisitive American eyes
Into your towns & towers.
So be good now, old gentleman.

Arrival at Malta. 2nd February.
& quarantine. First visit by

The headmaster, the cards presented
On the end of long poles

By the grocer & ship chandler,
Then the Spenditor's clamor,

Then by Paul Enyaud, merchant signor.
Night in the Parlatario,

I converse across the barriers
With Germans, Greeks, Maltese & Turks,

Sicilians, Moors & Englishmen.
Among them roam the friars

& guards, the poor & the maimed.
Such grotesque visages!

It resembles more an antique portrait
Than a room of flesh & blood.

My curiosity is distinctly European:
All darker cousins

Do not so much as cast a second glance,
Whereas we (myself & my Anglican brothers)

Stare in wonderment at the delightfully exotic
Clothes & faces, unable to tear our ears

From their musically inscrutable words.

Stonetown, a box of curiosities.
In St. John's Cathedral, the verger
Leads me into a darkened vault,

Air perfumed by marble & dust
& a frozen quality where
Fleeting time slows to a crawl

& the true age of the world
Is discerned when stripped
Of greenness. L'Isle Adam,

Grand Master of the Knights
Of St. John, who was given Malta
By Charles V, lies buried here,

As does La Valetta, who defended
The isle against the Sultan.
Perhaps the day will come

When no one will remember them,
Or any longer care, & this tomb
Will finally fulfill its purpose
With the same rarefied air.

A few beautiful faces in the dancing crowd
& a beautiful face is worth going far to see.

That which is finest in beauty is moral
& the attraction of a long descended maiden

Is a sort of wild virtue, wild & fragrant
As the violets that surprise the mind,
Meeting divinity amidst flowers & trifles.

In the country of a crumbled arch
We see the place where Cicero

Found the globe & cylinder, the tomb
Of Archimedes. I hold my breath in awe.

On stone benches, all that's left
Of the theaters here, we gaze down

Upon the city & its harbor.
Poor Syracuse, diminished

Into shabbiness. Once its people
Numbered 800,000 & every time

A Sicilian lost sight of Minerva
He tossed honey, wheat & flowers

Into the sea. Dion, Timoleon,
Archimedes & Cicero among them.

The people here are good witnesses
To the past. They sense a hidden weight
Behind each act. They move as if
Some unseen principle discloses
The way tomorrow should unfold

& yet the utility of their acts
Disturbs me & makes me wonder
If perhaps it is humanity's condition
To disown its past, to forget its implications –

The fountain of Aretheuse
Being used as a wash basin.

In the Capuchin gardens, the monk
Takes us to an arch under which
Athenian prisoners recited the verse

Of Euripedes in exchange for their life.
& they say verse is of no practical value or use.
From there, the monk leads us inside

The convent & feeds us bread, olives & wine.
I tell the Padre I would stay here forever
If they would only offer me a room.

The river Anupis,
A narrow puddle,
About an oar's length,
Fabled in Cyane's song –

There Proserpine
Gathered flowers
& no wonder.
They number in the thousands.

Signor Ricciardi of Syracuse gives me
A letter to Padre Anselmo Adorno,
Celleraio of the monastery at St. Agatha
In Carania, which sits at the base

Of Aetna, a monument & a warning.
The vows of poverty & humility
Cost these monks nothing.
Its walls adorned with famous paintings,

The organ that imitates, sackbut & psaltery
Beneath its buried maker.
Gazing upon its many wonders,
I begin to think the architects

Of American churches have never seen
Those of Europe, or they would not
Be content with such simple edifices.
The Puritan restraint at work I suppose.

There's scarcely a house in sight
That does not bear a cross or inscription.
My companions laugh at my cracked Italian,
Correcting me at every opportunity
With a smile & hearty slap to the back.

They are very kind. At night, we drink
Together, & their camaraderie is such
That it puts the quiet & restrained meals
Of home to shame, the habits of a mean
& cold-blooded brood. They raise

Their voices when they agree &
Speak musically & to the stars
When emotion overcomes them,
Gesticulating with wild palms,
Flagrant movements that are as much a language

As the words they speak, words
Of such musical ostentation, rhythmic,
Alliterative & fluid, it seems its own poetry.
It is difficult to tell where a cordial hello
Becomes a line from Dante.

Capuchin convent, utter humility compared
With the Benedictine monastery.
To reach their houses you must walk through a regiment
Of beggars. While the fathers are at dinner,

I pass the time walking in their somber garden.
A monk arrives, at first mistaking me
For one of his brethren, due to my dark coat
& sober countenance. He shows me

To their cemetery, long aisles of walls
Both sides of which are carved niches,
Whereby are lain the human remains
Of former Capuchins, wrapped in garments

Save for their hands & the head,
Some of which still have their beards or hair,
So fresh were their remains. In my silence
The monk beside me speaks with reverence:
"Someday I will join them here, God willing."

Naples. Another place of froth,
Cake & ale. Europe casts its spell:
It is easy for the traveler to be dazzled
By its stately arrangements, meant to impress
By the immense regard which is given
To clean shoes & smooth hats –

One's concentration is shattered by these
Distracting particulars. Better plain
Old Adam, the simple self against
The whole wide world, insisting
Upon his right to judge & see.

I find Goethe the perfect antidote
To ostentation. Nothing else so soothes
The soul. In my black lodgings
In the Croce di Malta, I & G
Chase the empty hours approaching sleep.

At Virgil's tomb, assailed by the cry
Of urchins, I look through its aperture
Into the Grotto of Posilippo, to the bright
& beautiful country of vineyards
& olive groves beyond to Canaldoli,
The ruins ruined by beggars.

Pompeii at dawn. The rebuilt city
Opened to the sun 1,700 years
After its burial in volcanic ash.

Our guide walks us through the remains
Of this Roman city, its baths & bath-houses,
Its prisons & temples, & I read

The inscriptions & scribbles on the wall
As if written mere months before.
I examine the frescoes, red & yellow

& the marble baths of private houses.
The utensils have been removed to Naples
& to Sicily. What a pity not to find them here.

It would have lent an impressive immediacy
To this spectacle of sudden death, this window
Into an unalterable & tragic past.

Thence we climbed with good staves
Thro' loose soil composed of lava & cinders,
Wind blowing smoke & fumes in the face.

At the top, we looked down into the smoking pit
Glowing red & yellow. I imagine
A chasm of unknown depth

& not this hollow of sulphur & salt.
We place paper between the stones
& they light immediately in flame.

Descending, we encounter another party
Ascending, their ladies carried in chairs.

The dying Gladiator, the Venus de Milo,
The Antinous, then to the Tarpeian Rock,
Then to the vast & spending Vatican,
A wilderness of marble, where I saw
The Apollo & Laocoön.

He who has not seen them cannot know
What beautiful stones are on the planet.

In Rome, all is ruinous.
In the garden before my window
Flowerpots stand upon blocks

Made of capitals of old columns
Turned upside down.
Everywhere, the walls & foundations,

Fragments of carved & fluted stone
Are found, once the ornament
of Vesta, or Jove.

In the Sistine Chapel
To see the Pope
Bless his palms
& hear his choir
Chaunt the passion –

It is difficult to see
The gentle son
Who rode upon an ass
Amidst the cries
Of his fickle followers –

The Pope's eyes
Closed as he rides –
To the Indian's sight
This must be ridiculous,
The mutilated sing.

Thy God,
The Unattainable –

Neither here nor heritage –

How effervescent & superficial
Is most of that emotion
That Art or Magnificence can awaken.

The large cathedrals
Are largely veneer.

The artist's rags & canvases,
The dingy squalor of his studio
Contrasts pathetically with
The grandeur of his finished work.

Difficult to imagine Caesar fell
At the feet of the Pompeii statute,
Whose sculptor perished
In poverty & anonymity –

What hope is there for wealth
& fame & the accolades
Of the people when all one has
To offer is beauty & form.

It cannot matter to the diseased
Or the banker, a diversion
Or decoration to please the eye –
Yet how many of them fail!

3 Apr. Wednesday.
The Misière in the Sistine Chapel.

The Emperor of Austria
Sent Mozart to Rome

To learn the choir's sound
So that it might be performed

In Vienna with like effect,
Yet he failed.

Good Friday. The Mystery of Tre Ore,
Processions in the streets, death's heads

Mounted on black staves, the great
Coliseum in moonlight, full of dread.

St. Peter's Church, an ornament
Of the earth, grief that I shall see it
No more. Walked the grounds
Of the Villa Borghese
Whilst the birds sang to me.

Silver river, tinged with regret
Over days escapes without my eye,

Drinking in the wild light
Or my skin caressed by ocean breeze.

Byron was right to fix his vision
On this place, to make beauty

& ruin his muse, the justness
Of his thoughts, the defects

Of his Harold. Walking past
The tomb of Machiavelli

Without glancing, I stop
Before Galileo's grave with veneration.

Then to the empty tomb of Dante,
Who lies buried at Ravenna.

The wax Plague of Florence,
A description of how man
Is made & destroyed,
An accurate copy of every organ

& process in the human frame.
It is beautiful & terrible
For nature did not intend
These things to be revealed.

A country of ornaments,
Vine & strawberry
Flower in hat or buttonhole,
Peacock's feathers,
Ornate designs
On the cripple's crutch,
Fountains & pumps
Like the finest carved sculpture,
Red a favorite color –

Rainy morning at Messina,
The streets ablaze
With bright umbrellas.

A damp Last Supper
Spoiled by time
In candle light
In the dim recesses
Of the Church San Domenico.

Yet Christ's face remains
Freshly strange,
Quiet & mysterious,
In possession of an unspeakably
Terrifying secret wisdom.

The poorest among them
Live in good houses,
Small palaces –
So unlike the hovels
Of their unfortunate American brethren.

Dining with workers
In a room filled with frescoes,
Its previous owners
Gone on to more recent fortunes.

Near the town at the foot of the Alps
Domo d'Ossala,
We pause before ascending
Via the road cut by Bonaparte.

Passing the ragged variations
Of rock, from the hot
Plains of Lombardy
To the chilled snowbanks
Of Sempione, the brief hamlet
Which crowns the top –

Here we stop,
Admire our breath
Visible in the night air,
& warm ourselves
Beside a thick fire
In a cozy inn,
Empty of travelers.

The weight of history
Infuses every sliver
Of wood, each silver utensil,
& I easily imagine
A similar inn
Occupied by almost
Ancient ancestors, clothed
In bearskin & leather
& these I think are the mountains
Of freedom,
Proving moral efficiency
Among Swiss peasantry.

At Gibbon's garden
At Lausanne I pluck a lime tree leaf
& acacia as my guide shows me
This landscape of which
Gibbon seemed so very proud.

France changes more than a name –
Nothing here is the same as in Italy.
The ongoing argument is over
& all are accommodating.

The country is a vast, undulating
Champlaign without a hill,
Planted like the Connecticut intervals,
The fields full of working women.

Crossing the Seine, the disappointments
Of Paris begin: nowhere here the air
Of antiquity & history. It is more
Like an abused New York.

Yet they greet the foreigner
With interest & humor. One merely
Presents his passport & the doors
Of the Sorbonne are flung widely open.

Père Le Chaise – a vain nation,
These French. The tombstones
Are *advertisements*. Yet

Many are affecting:
A dark slate stone "Mon père"
"Ci git" preferable to "ici repose" –

In the morgues the police expose
The bodies of the drowned,
That they may be claimed
By family or friend.

A suite about the Palais Royal –
Commerce est magnifique,
While churches are beggardly & mean.

Streets swarm
With journals & books
& every corner
Forms a little library,
An orchestra of discourse –

Company & newspapers
In the public rooms
& arcades –

Dazzling shops, costly luxury.

Mosquito in amber,
A cabinet of curiosities
Among the birds of paradise –

The ibis, the sacred & the rosy –
Ah, said I, this is philosophy,
A universe of bewildering puzzles,

Hazy butterflies & carved shells,
Life in the rock,
The centipede inside,

The skills collected there.
The English seems best –
Balenta like a capsized schooner,

Noah's Ark in the flower garden.
The stately giraffes, the mammoth
Yet cordial elephants.

The shell's knot & spine, the lip of structure,
The magnet wheels north
& clings to iron like one alive –

A universe
Constructed –
Harmonious & perfect –

All classification arbitrary & yet
In all the permutations & combinations
Might not a cabinet of shells
Retain its beauty
If not examined apart?

The glimmering of that pure, plastic Idea –

The etymologist no better than a titmouse
Peeping & darting after prey –
What Goethe sought in his metamorphosis of plants,

The Pythagorean doctrine of transmigration,
The Swedenborgian affections clothed.

Minute dissections,
The added acquaintance of intimate structure
Under sun & landscape –

Integrate the particulars –

The apparations of ethical truths
& natural classifications
Already their place & fate.

Goethe's arch, all possible vegetable forms
Gives birth to Beasts & Dreams.

Boulogne by steamship for London
A rough twenty hours. Up the Thames,
So familiar from maps & traditions,

The old city, vast & still.
The city streets empty.

Docked at St. Paul's then walk
Through Cheapside, Newgate,
To lodgings at Russell Square.
To hear again a familiar tongue –

The joy of it, & to let them be
& not wonder aloud
Our opinion of every person,
We meet, good Englishmen all.

My God, on the sea among strangers
To this hour, resist the evil
That is within evermore
In the consciousness.

Industry unsinking
& unconquerable –

Up the Forth by steamboat
For Stirling. Cold rainy wind
In our teeth all that way
Past Falkirk & I in my cabin
Quietly reading my book.

They put me in a little room aloft.
I was in no condition to dictate
& crept away to bed. Armed with razors

& clean shirt I recover courage
On a visit to the Cathedral of 1123,
Where, in the vaulted cellar is laid

The scene of part of Rob Roy.
My guide speaks Scotch but swears
Her name was not Deans.

Amid wild & desolate
Heathering hill
Without companionship
(save for his wife)
Carlyle speaks broad Scotch
With evident relish –
Ay, ay, & c. & c.

Gibbons' Bridge,
New York –
To old,
Plastic man,
Small on this vast earth –
Oceans between us
& torturous waves
Far beyond
Dry earth
Where naked feet
Once stood –
Where we now stand –

Our principle
Is not rebellion
Unless it is against
A cold & callous heart.

28 August 1833. Called upon Mr. Wordsworth.
His daughters bring him in & he sits
Across from me in goggles, speaking with
The greatest simplicity, mainly of America,
A society he deems enlightened by
A superficial tuition out of all proportion
To its being restrained by morality –

Schools do no good.
He speaks of Newton's laws as though
They were to be overturned.
He says "what is needed most in America
Is civil war to teach them the necessity
Of tying tighter the social bonds."
America's vulgarity, he insists, is a result

Of its pioneer state, yet the world
Is too much with them, there is a lack
Of class among its men of leisure.
Outside, in his garden, the place
Where he wrote his thousands of lines,
I look into his red & sour eyes
That no longer read words,

& since he writes no prose
His head carries a book's worth of verse
From which he freely quotes. They seem
So new, you'd think he'd newly improvised.
We walked over a mile, stopping
Every hundred paces or so
For him to quote a verse. His opinions
That of an old man who never aged past seventeen.

England, this Gibraltar of propriety,
A paradise of comfort & plenty,

Is, like Spencer's Bower of Bliss,
A false paradise where art conquers nature,

Where an ash-colored sky
Confounds night & day,

& smoke & soot
Make all times & seasons one hue,

Discolors saliva, poisons the air,
Corrodes monuments & buildings.

A terrible machine has possessed
These women & men

& hardly even a thought is free.
All is false & forged –

A cold, barren, almost arctic isle
Made luxurious through artifice.

To the English, a gesture upsets,
As it is almost a secret, a surprise,

A newness, a kind of traveler.
They wear faded wardrobes of the past,

They masquerade new lands
On marble floors where nothing grows.

Man's elasticity & hope
Must remain on the Allegheny ranges

Or nowhere at all.
In America, nature lies sleeping,

Almost conscious, & so gives
A certain *tristesse*,

Like the swamp's rank vegetation,
Or forests steeped in dew & rain.

In the sea-wide sky-skirted prairie,
It lies, driven away

From the trim hedge-rows
Of this over-cultivated island

Where everyone is on good behavior
& must be dressed for dinner by six.

Goethe, Newton, Gibbon – expert spinners
Of superficialities to hide the universe

Of our ignorance. Tho' poems & histories
Are expedients for bread & conceal

Boundless ignorance, there is Socrates' famous saying:
The recantation of man.

(Recitation)

God led me through this European scene,
From Malta's isle, through Sicily,
Through Italy, through Switzerland,
Through England & France,
& Scotland, in safety & pleasure,
& has now brought me to shore
& ship, steering westward.

She has shown me the men I wished to see
& has comforted & confirmed
My convictions. I owe many things
To the sight of these men.
I shall judge more justly, less timidly
Of the wise forevermore, to be sure
Not one of them is a first-class mind.

Deficient in differing degrees
To that species of moral truth
Which I call the first philosophy,
They feel themselves to be above
The meanness of pretending knowledge.
Men of genius speak sincerely
& will tell you freely what puzzles them.

But I am glad my travelling is done.
A man not old feels himself
Too old to be a vagabond.
The people at their work, the people
Whose vocations I interrupt,
Make you feel fame is a conventional thing
& that man is a sadly "limitary" Spirit.

You speak to them as to children
Whom it is necessary to humor,
Adapting one's tones & remarks
To known prejudices & not
To our knowledge of the truth.
It is better to admire too rashly
Than to be admired the same.

God save a great man from a circle of flatterers,
A sweet, very sweet ratsbane –
They miss by their premature canonization
Much necessary knowledge
& one of these days must begin the world again.

EMERSON IN AMERICA

It is an unworthy superstition for seers to go to Italy or France & come home & describe houses & things. Let them see men & magnify the passages of common life.

EMERSON, *JOURNALS*, 1833

Sea, 1833. Fair fine wind
In sight of land.
This morning, 37 sail in view.

I wish I knew where & how I ought to live.
But no moralities now,
The good, the holy day –

The sea breaks in the bulwark of ships –
Butterfly or log –
Pitch & rock –

The tempest roars,
Ropes snap, spars crack –
Our eyes upon Cicero or Addison in our hands –

Yet the noise of life touches us
In the pathless valleys of the sea,
In this human art the ship.

Tides break in the shallows,
Crevicing sands,
The silent delineaments
Of the island's erasure,
The mountain submerged,
Flowers & greenery consumed
By the ocean's chasmic maw.

Charmed by the color & forms of the shell,
I picked them up & placed them in my pocket.

When I returned home, I found nothing
Of what I gathered, just ugly mussels & snail shells.

Then I learned that Composition
Is more important than forms.

On the shore they lay, wet & social by the sea.

At Mount Auburn,
Luncheon at Fresh Pond,
A whole bed of Anemones,
Blue & beautiful –

A black-capped titmouse
Comes upon his tree.
Sings *chick-a-dee-dee*.

I forsake the tombs
& find a sunny hollow
Where the east wind could not blow
& open my eyes
& let pass through them
Into the soul.

Only noble earth
& the great Star that warms innumerable green needles
Of glittering pines
& the drab oak leaves
Turn their little somersaults
& lay still again.

You shall ray out light & heat,
You shall know absolute good,
Superfluous rules,
The enormous apertures
Overlaid & killed
& compass, land & sea
& nearer nearest –

A few few hours in the longest life
Is very little life
In a lifetime.

I look at the Almanack affectionately
As a book of promise.
The last three years of my life are not a chasm –

Hold up this lamp & look back
At the passages you have undertaken:

"I consult the auguries of time
& through the human heart,
Explore & look & listen."

The plough displaces the spade,
The bridge the watermen,
The press the scrivener –

Yet how seldom the present is seized upon
As a new moment – & man is seldom alone
Unless thrown against the stars.

A prophet is always preparing
A penitentiary for angels.
Rich wisdom hidden
In the dust & decay
Coughs & sputters
In the utter collapsing dark.

Some duties are above courtesy.
Solemnity prevails. Prayers distress
The withheld world,
The weariness of a delicious day
Touched by celestial fingers,
Puppets or potentates –

The creator's clearinghouse
Obscures & obfuscates –
Unwieldy design –
A waterhouse of confusion & pain,
The spirit overlaid & lost,
Or worse, collected into books.

We walk equally
Practiced roads
In restless charity,

We bow to the merchants
Who scrape the native cities,
Their trade a bubble

Built upon a bubble
& without end –
A work of arithmetic,

Adding voyage to voyage,
Stock to stock,
Dexterity in particulars,

Their arms remote.
If this perilous world
Were made solid

It would fit in a nutshell –
Books are an errand
Of the ignorant & profane –

The wise passage of genius,
Whose infinite conclusions
Are his confessions.

Goethe's nothingness:
The eye to conceal the Universe
Of Ignorance –
Poems expedients for bread,
Or to keep from the madhouse.

The undersong of confession
& infinite amazement –
Questions fended off
By the writing of books –
Profound calculations –

The gestures of reason,
Profoundly incalculable –
The uplifted eye of Memory,
Another dream of nature
Errored by right thinking.

Call your vulgar man,
Your prosy, selfish sensualist,
& awaken God & shake the world.

Something holy & wise
Will sit upon all countenances,
A playground to a child

& the hours shall shine
With a wisdom not their own
& the past will lie down in the basements of the heart.

In desert lands, the bird alights
On the barrel of a hunter's gun –
The wise must be wary & the gifted should advance

Only a single step,
Lest they be left without confidence
In their conductor.

To count the awful powers
In this sober solitude of woods –
I will listen then & speak.

An insect fertilizing dirt with worm casts,
A buzzard performing beneficence
Cannot hinder if it would.

Hawks wheel in spiral flight heavenward,
Each circle becoming less to the eye

As the bird vanishes into the vault of sky –
That grand observatory of barnyards,

Field mice & moles, so with the pelican crane
& sea-fowl tribes, greedy eaters,

Disgusting gluttons all, yet how finely into nature
They integrate a clean & pleasing whole.

Ask wrens & crows & bluebirds –
Returning to shells
The size & color of the moon
As to a dinner plate,
& so the world renews its race
For a thousand summers –

To know nature
Is to grasp a kind of permanence –

Clouds & grass, antiquities
Older than pyramids –
Goethe's plant-genuine creation –

To see a cistus or a brentus
Is to sigh with ignorance
Beyond mere classification.

The Vast Eternity opens before you,
A rich abyss, mute & void,

Demanding something god-like
In him that casts off common yokes & motives –

High be his heart,
Be it a world, or simply purpose.

The best sermon
Is quiet conversation –

Difficulties, discords,
To show the chain under the leather –

Silence: where the heart finds its wisdom,
In the darkest maze amid the sweetest baits –

The little needle finding North.
The bird remembering its note.

Empty oration.

Animals have been called
'The dream of nature'

& in our dreams
We conceive their consciousness,

We assent to the Monstrous,
We glimpse calamity.

The rare women
Take possession of society –

To them the whole earth
Is a cultivated garden,
Given form, given tone –

If they sit as we sit to wait
For what must be said
We shall have no Olympus –

Their genius is elegance.
While men stammer & mince,
They speak simply as song.

"We love good as much as any Englishman.
We too know what is kind, what is great.
When you first came to us from the morning waters,
We took you into our open arms.
We thought you children of the sun.
Now we are told that the country
Spreading far from the sea
Is passed away to you forever – perhaps for nothing –
Because of the names & seals of our sagamores,
They never turned their children from their homes
To suffer: their souls were too great."

The abomination of desolation
Is not a burned town
Or a country wasted by war.

It is the discovery that the man
Who has moved you
Is an enthusiast upon calculation.

Society is extinct, Carlyle proclaims.
So be it. It existed in Alaric & Atilla's time,

In the Crusades, in Puritan conventicles.
I prefer solitude now to society then,

For true solitude exists only where there is love.
Society's for caterpillars. Butterflies fly alone.

It is easy in the world to live
By another man's opinions.
It is easy in solitude to be
Self-centered. But the finished man
Is he who in the crowd
Keeps with perfect sweetness
The independence of solitude.

I knew a man of simple habits
Who never put out his hand,
Nor opened his lips
To court a reputation –
Honor came at last
& sat down with him
From which he has never stirred.

First thoughts, God's thoughts,
But not numerically first.
Allow what space you may
For the mind to group the facts,
Then thoughts achieve divinity.

Yet the devout old men of the cloth
Continue to question intelligence.
If only St. Paul would come
& replace these threadbare rags,
This sucked eggshell orthodoxy,

This false reverence from Jesus
That mistakes the stream for the source.
God is every man. All noble hearts
Converse & speak of the universe
& testify the truth.

Too much philosophy
& the world goes to sand.
Quam parva sapientia.

Natural history is without value,
But marry it to human history
& it becomes poetry.

The plant's habit, the sound
Of a hurried insect –
Human nature is beautiful?

To some degree.
King Lear is beautiful –
That wretched & pitiable scream

Of a naked & broken man,
A king confronted by a fool, himself,
Sturdying himself with rage.

The people, the people –
You hold up your pasteboard religion
For those unfit for truth.

So you say. Yet there will arise
A race of preachers
Who will take hold of truth's omnipotence

& will blow old falsehoods to shreds
With their breaths.
No poem is so musical as the law

Of compensation, when an ardent mind
Glimpses perfect beauty
& it envelops him

& determines all his being –
Will he return to periodic shouting
About atoning blood?

We sit down with intent to write
Of truth & end up with a book
Containing no thought of ours
But the music of time, its waste

& its passing. We have nothing
But the false schedule of eternity.
The book I thought might say
What I choose for it & yet

It seems now a sort of *fata morgana*,
Reflecting better poets, men
More knowledgeable than I
& of a more learned tongue,

Whose minds are a continent,
While mine must contend
With the humble habitation
Of a few desolate plots.

The excellent are all very much alike.
They awake with the desire to unfold
All the most delightfully profound

& simple facts, in somber tones,
With well-chosen words,
A tapestry of truth brought to us

The way a laborer brings with him
His lunch to work. We stand dumbstruck
In awe at the inscrutable apparatus of genius.

It seems impractical
To never arrive at the right moment.
It must be difficult

When every cell screams stay alive –
How to shake off that unquenchable breath?
How, finally, to quit.

The doctors pulled the old patient aside
&, speaking loudly in his ear, said:
"You must simply give *in*."

The noise of the bee
& the light in the pines,
Butterflies & spiders,
The tints & forms
Of the leaves & trees –
Seeds & capsules,
Asters & polygalas,
& overhead the eternal sky.

Beauty is right action,
Nature a seedbox of vision –
Events unspool
As the arc of the wheel's curve
Arrives full circle,
No closer to completion
Than the infinite.

An open eye discovers much
In every passenger –
An upward glance starkly reminds one
Of the frozen infinitude of space,
Of the cold, empty, breathless expanse –

Nevertheless you must insist on yourself.
Never imitate. For your own talent
You can present every moment
With all the force of a lifetime's cultivation,
But of the adopted stolen talent
You have only a frigid brief extempore half-possession.

Adhere to your own & produce it
With the meek courage that intimates
This possession is my inheritance.

Received tidings of death.
Again the grim guest makes his guaranteed appearance.
Death my dear brother
On this first day of the month
At St. John's, Porto Rico.
So falls one more pile of hope for this life.

"Whatever fortunes wait my future life.
The beautiful is vanished & returns not."

Thou art quiet in thy grave.
The dead are happier than the living.
In thy rivulets,
In thy movements of time,
Wrapped in a shroud forever safe,
Laid sweet in the grave of human hope,
In the tumults of the Natural World.

It is a massive step from the thought
To the expression of the thought

In action. Without horror
I contemplate the envy, hatred, & lust

That occupies the hearts
Of smiling well-dressed men & women,

Yet the simplest most natural expressions
Of the same thoughts in action

Astonish & dishearten me.
If the wishes of the lowest class

That suffers in these long streets
Should execute themselves,

Who can doubt that the city
Will topple into ruin.

History: What man suffers & believes.
The slowness with which
The *stirps generosa sea historica*
Opened their eyes
To the monstrous lie of Popery
Might startle us
To the depths of degradation,
Through the sleep of reason
& the hopes of heights
We might attain –

Luther, Coleridge says, acted poems
& their sublime is the material sublime –
Mahomet's description of the Angels:
Nine days journey from eye to eye.

Sublimity of magnitude & number –
"Where the heart is not moved,
The gods stride & thunder in vain.
The pathetic is the true sublime."

Ah, how shone the moon & her little sparklers –
There was light in the selfsame vessels
Which contained it a million years ago.

What, is this lone parsonage in this thin village
So populous as to crowd you & overtask
Your benevolence? Arises the idea of God

Peopling the lonely places, effacing the scars
Of our mistakes & disappointments,
Firing the heart with the hardening of presence.

Judge for yourself:
Democracy's root & seed
Makes every man a state,
Places the dead with a check
In true delicate reverence
For superior minds.

"How is the king greater than I,
If he is not more just."

Society clothed with bodies –
Every dress, every house,
Every newspaper in every town,
Bricks & lathes & lime
Fly obedient to the mind.

Dawn breaks, the sun sets,
The dome's slate-colored clouds

Become a wreath of roses.
Or look down the river

Lined by trees, green & orderly,
A coronation of elegancy

As if in a dream.
Is this superficial?

Or is the Earth itself unsightly?
Narcissus, crocus, lily or petal,

An assemblage of bright & opake balls
Floating in space, each individual

A counterpart & contemplator of the whole.
Events shall shape the Earth,

Lie packed in silence, awaiting their birth.
Everything emerges, converges,

A pebble & cloud,
Scraps of thought & action.

Blessed are the woods.
In summer they shade the traveler from the sun,
In winter from the tooth of Wind.

When there is snow it falls level.
When it rains, it does not blow in his face.
There is no dust & pleasing fear reigns in their shade.

It was not that long ago
That men in distant countries
Were painted as monstrous bodies,
Reckless, with tails, & c.

But commerce contradicted these reports.
Then they were accused
Of possessing monstrous minds –
Thieves, sottish, promiscuously mixed –

Yet commerce exposed that slander
& shows that as a face
Answereth to a face in the water,
So the heart of man to man.

What is a man but a Congress of nations?
Deliver us from that intensity of character
Which makes all its crows swans.

Every fairy brings a gift, every trait, every trifle,
Every nothing is canonized & caricaturing.
It frets & confuses.

I rejoice in time.
I do not cross the common
Without a wild poetic delight.

No hour, no state of the atmosphere,
But correspondence to some state of mind:
Brightest day, grimmest night.

The eye was placed
Where the ray should fall

That it might testify
Of that particular ray.

On precocity & the dissection
Of the brain & the distortion

Of the body & genius,
A grim compost of blood & mud.

Cursed are those lost in their pursuits,
Who never knew they had a body.

A good sentence or verse
Is like a fine statue,

A beautiful cornice,
An Oxford staircase,

A noble painted head.
One writes on the air

If he speaks, but
He writes on a mind

More durable than marble
& begets Nations,

Launches out from the Infinite
& builds roads into Chaos.

As the love of flowers contains Botany,
So nature makes a poet of every boy –

The same desire of the untried
Leads the young farmer to load his wagon
& rattle down the long hills toward Illinois.

The chickadees are busy
In Caesar's woods –
Between the spots of snow
I met them yesterday.

What is the green leaf
Under the ice
Resembling potentilla?

Philosophies are judged
By the standing or following
Of academes,

Yet no man lives or dies
By a professor's taste,
Which changes nothing,

Though they behave
Like the mere act of saying
Alters gravity & space.

It sees & declares
How laws advance –

Their reign forevermore
Into Infinitude –

Jesus & Socrates – spiritualists all –
While Fox & Penn are men of wraith.

I see the world & its maker
From another side.

Bottom – philosopher of the kidney –
Fathers each moment named.
It fills his whole horizon.

He mistakes omnivolence for omnipotence –
His only remedy a new thought
To withdraw him from the last.

What must be said in a lyceum?
Fragmentary lopsided mortals
Assembling to the heavens,

The soul endowed with the poetry of affliction
To whom a starved worm reeks
Of the bounty of heaven –

Compassion – who speaks of compassion?
Those that decorate the galleries,
Open their doors, offering free admission,

So that the child that hungers might know
That beyond the grimy tenement windows
Lie heaven's sublime visions.

Light makes beautiful
Every object in nature

& none loses beauty
By being nearer seen.

Snow & moonlight makes all landscapes alike.
Everything may be painted, everything sung

But to be a poem
Its feet must be lifted from the ground.

The wind will go down with the sun,
Leafless trees will become spires of flame

& the stars of dead calices of flowers
& every withered stem rimed with frost

With all their forms & hues
Contribute to the mute music of the world.

How old is the pebble,
The magnet –

I consult the auguries of time,
Look at the Almanack affectionately –

The thing set down in words
Is not affirmed –

It must affirm itself –
This is the core of the world.

Evil times make men think.
Wise moments are years

Forever lighting the countenance.
They are good; they do not

Belong to genius, but to man.
They refuse to be recorded.

The eye that sees that all things are good,
Not of man, neither by men –

The round world loose
In the cold vacuum of space.

Mind is the first philosophy,
The science of what is

& not what appears to be.
The mark of astronomy

Contains the sphere,
Astonishes understanding

& gleams of a world
In which we do not live.

We have yet to devise
Words that can withstand
The perfection of intuition,
"The tumult of the soul" –

It is not, it will not be
The Sermon on the Mount –
Flawless utterance of the mind
Contemplating the world.

In the chambers of the street,
Wisdom's regions are unearthed –

How thin the veil.
A Lethean stream

Washes us through
& bereaves us of ourselves –

This common life
Of phantasms –

We dream of sand
& light breaking over the rocks.

I belong to mankind
& my wayward heart
Communes with worms –

Doves spread their angelic darkness
under the blue clouds
& smoke roams the cold corridors –

What an insect of death, the heart,
Wetly pressing the blood
From darkness to darkness.

I am open to the name of a loose speculator,
A faint, heartless supporter of a frigid
& empty theism, a God of no rigor
Of manners, of no vigor or *primum non nocere* –

How can we speak to the unpractical,
The middling, how do we speak to error,
How might we illustrate the harmony
& depth of their great circling truths?

Knowledge is difficult to achieve
& unsatisfying once possessed –
Utterance is enough in heaven, yet
In this world, only mind is known,

& the only economy of time
Is saying & doing nothing untrue
To the self, to live wholly within,
Possess no sacred law but Nature

& perceive one's commissions
Coeval with the eldest causes.

"The world in which I exist is another world indeed, but not to come."

                                                                                                       Coleridge

Here we stand before the manse –
The low, wooded hills,
The old Indian cornfields
& great meadows along the Concord,
& the light that ripples through the tall elms
& the light that drapes its eastern face
That pours warmth through the windows –

How must this house now seem
To those who stand before it,
How like monochrome ghosts we must appear
To that radiant image of the future eye –
How dreary & desolate the past
& how empty of its people.
How silent, & how deathly still.

Every truth is a full circle.
The words have a divine sound:
The music of a surly storm
That rocks the walls & fans my cheek
Through chinks & cracks –

The great willow tree over my roof
Is trumpet & accompaniment
Of this raucous concert: It roars
Like the rigging of a ship in a tempest
& I sing my strain though hoarse & small.

Lime to clothe the bones of the dead

Bricks to build the corpse of religion

Books to bury human utterance

Greed to rage at nature's parsimony

Love to confuse the world's brutality

Words to stifle the mind's thunderous vocabulary

As poor as I am rich,
I shall parade my rags

Before the throne of God,
Emblems of my suffering,

To show him I did not fail from want.
& when the stones go blind

Contemplating the sudden death of our sun
& the oceans & all the wandering graceless tribes

Of living things lay down
In a furnace of ice

To greet the avenging spirit
Who draws from us our last labored breath

& places it against his heart,
In the cold throne of the firmament

I shall carry the stone
That bends its hands

To the warmth that sparks
All startled creation.

Riding east to Sudbury, I am pleased
With the beauties & terrors of the snow,

& the oak leaves hurrying over the banks
Are a fit ornament. Nature in my woods

Is companionable, reason is sufficient
company. I have my glees & glooms,

I have my dead & absent again,
& contend alone for a thousand years.

I know no aisle so stately as the roads
Through the piney woods of Maine.

How intense our affinities:
Acids & alkalis, affections indulged –

The earth metamorphosises, all tragedy
& ennui vanish, all duties even –

Were I assured of meeting Ellen tomorrow
Would it be less than a world,

A personal world? Death has no bitterness
In the light of that thought.

ERIC HOFFMAN is the author of numerous books of poetry including *Forms of Life*, *By the Hours*, and *The American Eye*. His prose and poetry have been published throughout the world. Together with Dominick Grace, he has edited three volumes of the University Press of Mississippi's Conversations with Comic Artists series. He lives in Connecticut with his wife Robin and son Sailor.

www.ingramcontent.com/pod-product-compliance
Lightning Source LLC
Chambersburg PA
CBHW020935090426
42736CB00010B/1152